# ECHOES OF EMOTION
Javier Rhoden

Echoes of Emotions copyright ©2024 by Perseveerance.
All rights are reserved.
No part of this book may be reused or reproduced
In any manner without written permission
Except in cases of reprints in contexts of reviews.
Illustrations from Canva.

*Perseveerance*

# Echoes of Emotions

Also by Javier Rhoden
Luminescence
Lamentations
Altschmerz
Twilight Zone
Panorama

Acknowledgement.

I am forever grateful for the love and support that has been given to me by my wife, my two boys and her family. Their unwavering devotion and selflessness have been a constant source of inspiration, comfort, and joy throughout my life.

To my wife, I want to express my deepest gratitude for the endless encouragement and unwavering belief in me. Through the ups and downs, you have remained my constant support, my confidant, and my partner in all that we do. Your love has been a guiding light in my life, and I couldn't be more blessed to have you by my side. Thank you for everything, my love.

To my boys, I want to express how much joy and pride you both have brought into my life. Watching you grow and evolve into the amazing boys you are today has been one of the greatest pleasures of my life. Your sense of humor, kindness, and intelligence inspire me each and every day. You have made me a better person, and I am forever grateful for that.

Together, you both have filled my life with so much love, happiness, and purpose. I am blessed to have you in my life, and I will always be grateful for the impact you have made on me. Thank you for being my family, my companions, and my friends.

Synopsis

Distance may test the strength of a relationship, but it can never diminish the depth of true love.

TRUE.

There is no such thing as a perfect relationship. Every long-term partnership comes with its own set of challenges and issues. However, what sets a successful relationship apart is the willingness to work through those obstacles together. It takes continuous effort, patience, and dedication to keep a relationship strong. But in the end, the growth and love that comes from persevering through tough times with your partner makes it all worth it. A true relationship is built to last, not because it is perfect, but because the two people involved choose to make it work every single day until it accumulates to years.

LOVE STORY.
In the embrace of a lifetime's devotion,
A love story unfolds with pure emotion,
A tale of two souls entwined in grace,
A husband's love for his cherished embrace.
Like a gentle breeze on a tranquil shore,
Her love embraces him, forevermore,
A beacon of light in the darkest night,
His wife, his muse, his guiding light.
With each passing day, their love does grow,
Like a river's current, it continues to flow,
Through stormy seas and tranquil tides,
Their love withstands, forever abides.
In her laugh, he finds solace and delight,
Her smile, a beacon, gleaming so bright,
Her touch, a caress that soothes his soul,
Her presence completes him, makes him whole.
No words can capture the love that they share,
For it transcends realms, beyond compare,
In her eyes, he sees his reflection,
A mirror of love, with no imperfection.
In her, he finds peace, tranquility too,
A love that is pure, strong, and true,
She is the sun that lights up his sky,
His compass, his anchor, as time passes by.
In her arms, he finds comfort and release,
His sanctuary, where his worries cease,
Her presence, a soothing balm to his heart,
Their love, a masterpiece, a true work of art.
Through highs and lows, together they stand,
Hand in hand, united by love's gentle hand,
He cherishes every moment, every breath,

For in his wife's love, he finds life's endless depth.
So, let the world witness this love so rare,
A wife cherished beyond compare,
In the depths of his heart, her love will stay,
Forever cherished, until their dying day.

CHANGE.
I think bad habits play out from a lack of involvement
Being involved comes with no requirements but to be there
Everything else comes in the moment with outcomes lessening problems depending on how you solve them
It's why we suffer but the sharing of experiences is what makes the next person suffer less
I hope my words have you suffer less
And this is just one lesson I've learned from being a new father, there is no more
"I can't be bothered"
So its time to make changes

## MY WIFE.

In verses sweet, I'll praise her gentle grace,
The beauty of my wife, a sacred sight.
With eyes that sparkle like the stars in space,
Her radiant smile, a beacon of light.
Her touch, a balm that soothes my weary soul,
Each gentle caress, a tender embrace.
Her love, a warmth that makes me feel whole,
Her nurturing heart, a sacred space.
In every step, her grace unfolds with grace,
Her elegance, a dance upon life's floor.
Her presence, like a calm and gentle breeze,
Fills me with peace and leaves me wanting more.
Oh, wife of mine, your love like a dove's flight,
I'm forever blessed by your nurturing light.
As I penned the words to paint her grace,
Her beauty radiates, like a morning sun.
Her nurturing love, a guiding embrace,
In darkness, like a beacon, she's my one.
Through weary nights and storms that try hearts true,
Her love, like shelter, embraces my fears.
She nurtures with a kindness so accrue,
A flowing river, washing away tears.
Her touch, a remedy to aching soul,
Soft whispers heal wounds, deep and unseen.
Her presence, like a garden in full bloom,
Filling every corner, with love serene.
Oh, wife so fair, forever my beloved,
Your beauty and love, forever treasured.
In her eyes, I see oceans of love's depth,
A reflection of light that never wanes.
Her nurturing, like blossoms gently crept,

Fuels the fire within, as love sustains.
Her tender touch, a symphony of care,
Melodic whispers, healing all that's bruised.
She nurtures with a love beyond compare,
In her embrace, all pain and sorrow soothed.
Her presence, a sanctuary so divine,
A haven where my soul finds sweet respite.
In her arms, love's warmth forever entwined,
A nurturing love that guides me through night.
Oh, wife, my love eternally proclaimed,
Your beauty and nurturing love, untamed.

REMAIN OPEN.
Lately I've been heartbroken and that's because I've been heartspoken
Everything I've shared from a space I've remained open
I'd feel like I've misspoken
In this life you have to be taking notes and
If you haven't, then you haven't been taking notice
Of it's lessons from many sessions, we should know this

FOUNTAIN OF YOUTH.

Nectar drips from petals between your thighs, the ocean rise
From pores as waves crash underneath goosebumps of skin
Tones of love from our mouths is what we breathe in
The hour glass of time sits in curves of your hips
I'm reminded why loving you is so sublime moments with you inspires my muse and
I thank you for never making me feel like an island, forever
You are my fountain

PORTRAIT.
The stream of your legs go up
The mountain of your hips, it dips
Into the valley of your ribs, Which splits into two terrains from your back which show
You carry stars in your breasts with sun and moon fluorescing from your eyes
My love, you are the most breath taking portrait

COSMICALLY BEAUTIFUL.
Inside my wife's womb,
Violent tranquility,
Cosmic beauty blooms.

COSMIC HARMONY.
Oh, how I love to embrace my love this way
When she presents herself in perfect bliss,
Her rounded curves, they lead my mind astray,
And all I want to do is feel her kiss.
Her backside is a silent symphony,
A work of art that begs for my embrace,
A masterpiece of beauty, truthfully,
That leaves me in a state of endless grace.
I stroke her hair, I whisper in her ear,
And tell her how she's everything to me,
How I could never find another dear,
To love so much, so ardently, so free.
Our bodies move in cosmic harmony,
As I enter as the key to her heart

**JAVIER RHODEN**

## DIVINE.

My wife, my love, my everything divine,
Who brings to me such joy each passing day,
With her, my heart has found its place to shine,
And banished all my doubts and fears away.
She grips my hand and lifts me to the sun,
Her gentle smile, the beacon of my soul,
The laughter in her eyes, a joyous fun,
That makes my heart soar high to its rightful goal of true love

MY LOVE.
Her love is like a fountain of sweet bliss,
That quenches all my thirst and soothes my pain,
With her, my life is full and well-kissed,
And every moment spent with her is a gain.
My wife, the light that guides me through my strife,
My heart rejoices, for she's my love, my life.

WORK OF ART.
Her curves, a beating red heart,
Against my body, a work of art.
Our love, an unspoken oath,
As we move in passionate troth.
Fingers tangled in loose strands,
Moans escaping in passionate demands.
In this embrace, we are whole,
Uniting in body, a singular soul.

NEW FATHER.
Of all the joys that life may bring,
The sweetest by far is a newborn's first cling.
A father's heart expands with pride,
The moment he holds his newborn child.
Gone now the doubts and fears,
A new sense of purpose now appears.
With every coo and every smile,
Comes a newfound sense of worthwhile.
In your tiny face, I see hope and joy,
A miracle that no one can ever destroy.
As a father, I will strive to be the best,
To create a world where you feel the safest.
Your presence changes everything,
From the need to plan to your every little thing.
A profound love has sprouted within my heart,
Even at moments when you pull things apart.
I'm grateful for every moment spent in your care,
With every tiny step, it's love that we share,
This journey before me has just begun,
Becoming a father has made my heart truly won.
From this day forth, my purpose is clear,
To be a guiding light and a loving ear,
To make sure you soar fearlessly,
Into every dream, my shining galaxy.

NEW MOTHER.
The mother of my children
She glows with a radiance untold,
As my beloved, so bold,
Becomes a mother for our kids,
Her joy, like the rising sun, out-bids.
She cradles them with tender care,
And sings sweet lullabies in the air,
Her gentle touch, a soothing balm,
As she holds them close, safe from all harm.

## MOTHER'S LOVE.

I watch with awe, as she feeds,
Our little ones, fulfilling their needs,
Her selflessness, a shining gem,
A mother's love, a priceless emblem.
Her eyes sparkle with pure delight,
As they laugh and play, so bright,
Her heart overflowing with pride,
As she watches them grow, side by side

**MEMORIES.**
I thank the stars, for bringing us together,
And for this miracle, that we treasure,
For my wife, my partner, my muse,
For the mother she has become, I can't refuse,
To say, how much she means to me,
For all the love and care she has set free,
For the memories, we will forever hold,
Of seeing her, as a mother, so bold.

ROMANCE.
You are my everything
My moon, my sun, my stars
The rhythm in my heartbeat
The light in my darkened scars
My soul belongs to you
As we dance through this life
Hand in hand, heart to heart
Our love, our passion rife
I adore the way you smile
And the twinkle in your eye
The way you laugh and sing
Makes my heart soar up high
I cherish each moment with you
From the mundane to the sublime
You are my treasure, my joy
Our love a constant chime
No words can express
The depth of my love for you
My beautiful wife, my muse
My heart forever true

PRAISES. (Diamante)
Oh, she
Endowed love
Empathetic heart
Giving joy
Dedicated soul
Faithful spouse
Devoted life
...me

SECURITY.
Through understanding
My wife knows the essence of my heart
She speaks the language of my soul
I'm grateful to not be alone
Her love is a warm embrace that fills the spaces in my life
A love so true and pure
With her, I know my heart is secured forever

SAME SIDE.
Disagreements may happen in the heat of passion
Before regretful actions, remember
We're on the same side
And this should always be within our reasons

SOULMATE.
Her eyes once dutifully cold
Fearful of trusting and bold
But as our love slowly grew
Her heart learned to shine anew
My flaws, she accepted with grace
My quirks, a smile on her face
And with each passing day
Our love bloomed in its own way
Her heart once guarded and walled
Now freely given, completely enthralled
And in the embrace of her love's hold
All my doubts and fears were sold
For with her, my love, I am whole
In her arms, I find my soul.

**HEALING.**
Forgiveness blooms bright,
Releasing burdened hearts' weight,
Healing, peace in sight.

FORGIVING.

Forgiving heart beats,
Nature's embrace wraps around,
Time ticks slowly by,
My soul lives in her love's light,
Affection blooms evermore.

HEALING.
Forgiveness blooms bright,
Releasing burdened hearts' weight,
Healing, peace in sight.

## FORGIVING.

Forgiving heart beats,
Nature's embrace wraps around,
Time ticks slowly by,
My soul lives in her love's light,
Affection blooms evermore.

**LIFELINE.**
Cooking with love, care,
Warm hugs and tender embrace,
My wife, my lifeline.

HUSBAND.
I'm not a perfect husband but you have my heart
It aches me dearly to think back on the times I've hurt you
It's important for a man to control his anger
And the things that was said
I'm so sorry I've been venomous but I'm no stranger to owning up to my wrongs
Things take time
But two imperfect people refusing to give up on each other is how you find a version of a perfect marriage
Through thick and thin we can show our child what longevity means
Your presence brings healing as your love keeps my heart beating
I hope when you see me you see the reminder you have a friend forever
You are the nature of love in the flesh
I haven't felt that from any other
I am so proud you're my wife

MATURITY.
With a wife by my side, I have matured,
Gone are the days of reckless abandon,
No more wild nights with friends at the bar,
My love now a guiding force, my shining star.
Together we've faced the ups and downs of life,
Through good times and the strife of chaos,
Her unwavering presence, my anchor that lifts,
In moments of doubt and fears.
At times she is a burst of light,
Her laughter sparks my heart alive,
In her embrace, I find peace,
A refuge that is purely mine to keep.

TIME.
Our love deepened with every passing year,
A river of emotions, a bond that will never sever,
No matter the path we may go,
For the love we share, time will forever show.
Growing old with her, I realize that life is brief,
And we must cherish every day, every little relief,
Together we will face the end of time,
With her by my side, forever she'll be mine.
So as we mature and our love ripens with age,
With her, I am anchored through the darkest rage,
For every moment of doubt, she is my light,
My partner in life, my constant delight.

# JAVIER RHODEN

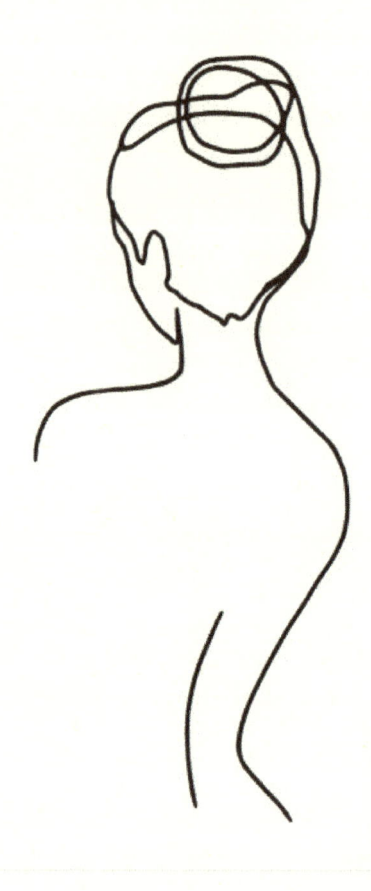

RAGING FIRE.
As I gaze upon your mesmerizing curves,
My passion for you inwardly surges,
Your perfect form, a work of art,
Stirring within me a blazing heart.
Your eyes, two pools of deepest brown,
Reflecting the love that we have found,
Your lips, full and supple, a thing of beauty,
Calling me to taste their sweet fruity.
You are the embodiment of desire,
Every inch of you, my soul's raging fire,
My love for you, a passion true and raw,
A never-ending flame, an unbreakable awe.
Your body, a temple that I long to praise,
Your every move, a sensual ballet,
Your scent, like a subtle perfume,
Captivating me like a sweet tune.
Oh, how I long to hold you tight,
All through the night, under candlelight,
To kiss and caress you, to show you my love,
And for another moment, I'll never get enough.
You are my queen, my heart, my soul,
I desire you more than any other goal,
My love for you, unwavering and true,
And forever, I'll cherish all that's within you.

NEVER ALONE.
My wife, my love, my saving grace,
Her presence gives me endless grace,
Through thick and thin, she's by my side,
A beacon of light, through every ride.
She works all day, without a single rest,
For her family, she gives her absolute best,
She cooks, she cleans, she cares for us all,
Her love, like a never-ending haul.
Her gentle smile, a ray of sunshine,
Her unwavering strength, like a steady line,
Through every challenge, she supports me true,
And in every moment, her love rings through.
She's always there to lend a hand,
A comforter when things aren't grand,
She lifts me up, when I'm feeling low,
And with her love, my heart does glow.
She's my soul mate, my life's treasure,
And every day, my love for her grows with pleasure,
Her touch, a sweet soothing balm,
Her voice, a calming song that keeps me calm.
My wife, my queen, my everything,
My constant in a world forever changing,
I pray that I'll always do right by her,
And honor her every day as my absolute honor.
For all her love, for all her care,
I thank her now and every year,
My wife, my love, my heart's true home,
Forever and always, you are never alone.

STRENGTH.
Verse 1:
She's a force of nature, wild and free,
A mystery that can't be tamed or solved easily.
She's a delicate flower, but don't be fooled,
Her strength will rise and her beauty will rule.
Chorus:
She's the embodiment of life,
The epitome of beauty and strife,
With a heart full of love and grace,
She'll light up any space.
Verse 2:
Her complexities are vast and deep,
An ocean of emotions that she'll keep,
She's the brightest sunshine and the darkest night,
A queen of contrasts, a magnificent sight.
Chorus:
She's the embodiment of life,
The epitome of beauty and strife,
With a heart full of love and grace,
She'll light up any space.
Bridge:
She'll fight for what she believes,
She'll love with all her might,
She's a warrior, she's a queen,
She's a beacon of light.
Chorus:
She's the embodiment of life,
The epitome of beauty and strife,
With a heart full of love and grace,
She'll light up any space.
Outro:

Her nature is a wonder to behold,
A mystery to unravel and unfold,
She's a precious gem, a rare find,
A woman like her is one of a kind.

FATHERHOOD.
Verse 1:
I used to think I had it all, life was grand,
But nothing can compare to being a dad, now that's a plan.
It ain't about the money, the cars, or the fame,
It's all about the love that fatherhood brings to the game.
Chorus:
Fatherhood, it's a different type of ride,
A journey that's filled with pride,
Gonna raise my kids and teach 'em right,
Through the ups and downs, we'll always fight.
Verse 2:
It's not about being perfect, we all make mistakes,
But fatherhood's a gift, it's never too late.
Gonna be there for my kids, always by their side,
Through the good times and the struggles, we'll always abide.
Chorus:
Fatherhood, it's a different type of ride,
A journey that's filled with pride,
Gonna raise my kids and teach 'em right,
Through the ups and downs, we'll always fight.
Verse 3:
I never knew love like this, it's a different sensation,
Gonna teach my kids respect, patience, and determination.
Gonna show 'em how to love, and how to be strong,
How to keep going, even when times are long.
Chorus:
Fatherhood, it's a different type of ride,
A journey that's filled with pride,
Gonna raise my kids and teach 'em right,
Through the ups and downs, we'll always fight.
Outro:

Fatherhood's a journey, a ride like no other,
Gonna be there for my kids, my sisters and my brothers.
Teach them right, love them true, show them what it's all about,
Fatherhood's a blessing, one that I won't ever lose clout.

ROOTS.
Verse 1:
I see the world around me, the chaos and the pain,
It's hard to keep moving forward, but we must all maintain.
Inequality and injustice, it's all around,
We gotta stand up and fight, make a true impact sound.
Chorus:
This is more than just a rhyme,
It's a message to the world that we gotta climb,
Together, stronger, towards a brighter day,
Gotta spread love and truth, it's the only way.
Verse 2:
I see the hunger and the thirst, the thirst for more,
We're chasing money and power, but what's it all for?
We gotta get back to our roots, connect with our souls,
Find our true purpose, and make our spirits whole.
Chorus:
This is more than just a rhyme,
It's a message to the world that we gotta climb,
Together, stronger, towards a brighter day,
Gotta spread love and truth, it's the only way.
Verse 3:
We gotta stop the hate and the violence, it's time to rise,
Come together as a people, and open our eyes.
It takes a village to raise a child, we all gotta do our part,
Spread love, not hate, and let it start from the heart.
Chorus:
This is more than just a rhyme,
It's a message to the world that we gotta climb,
Together, stronger, towards a brighter day,
Gotta spread love and truth, it's the only way.
Outro:

These are the message of my time,
Spread the love, spread the truth, let it shine,
Together we can make a change, that can't be denied,
So let's keep moving forward, let's continue to rise.

LOVE IS PATIENT. LOVE IS KIND.
If you seek some guidance for your relationship's course,
Listen up and heed this advice with force.
Communication and honesty should always be key,
Open to each other, love deeply, and you'll see.
Be patient and kind, even when things get rough,
Your love will flourish when things are tough.
Respect each other's space and freedom to grow,
Encourage each other to live life and flow.
Give compliments often and show your affection,
It's the little things that often hold each other's attention.
Embrace each other's flaws, love them as they are,
Find ways to evolve without leaving any scars.
Treat them like royalty, the one that you cherish,
Every moment with them, treasure and relish.
Compromise and forgiveness will set your hearts free,
For a happily ever after, these are the real key.
So listen to these words, take them to heart,
It takes two of you to make a work of art.
Keep the love alive and never let it go,
For the bond you share brings a beautiful glow.

PRESENCE.
I'm not a perfect father but you have my presence
It aches me dearly to think of times away from you
It brings joy to me when interacting with you
I can't feel blue when smiling at you too
It's important for a man to learn how to watch his behavior
And the things that he says
Don't become venom to genuine hearts
It's why I've stayed with your mother
Who's God's gift to me during times of chronic pain
This life I live is in an effort to leave better examples for searching people to pick up on
When I can no longer be called on
You can remember you are what you're searching for
I'm no celebrity and it was never a plan to be
Nor am I rich, nature has given me all I've needed for never playing the devils game
But I was fulfilled when I learned I was a father
Adiel and Eliel, you're the reasons I'm an author and more

FIRST BIRTHDAY.
To our little prince,
You are the most beautiful boy and it brings our heart joy
To lay eyes on you every morning when we wake up
You are full of life, emotion and love
One day you'll grow into a king and I hope the love your mother and I lavish you with is more than enough for you to be guided in this world.
Words cannot show how much we love you and how much you make us proud
Love,
Mom and dad

## GROWN UP.

You'll grow up to read this, you were young when I wrote this
Unborn when I was writing poetry in thought of you
Chronic pain couldn't keep me down I suit up and handle business
You can always call on me and your mothers my witness
Don't forget to call on your da-da
Its always going to be me and your mama

LETTER TO MY SONS.
As you journey through life,
I offer you some words of advice,
Some pearls of wisdom to help you thrive,
And guide you towards the path that's right.
Dream big and never give up on your goals,
Work hard and let tenacity be your soul,
Success awaits those who dare to pursue,
With passion, grit, and determination.
Stay true to yourself, your values, and beliefs,
Have the courage to stand for what is right,
Walk the path of integrity and honesty,
And let your actions be your guiding light.
Respect others and always show kindness,
Live with empathy and compassion for all,
Help where you can, and lend a hand,
For it is in giving that we find our call.
Take care of your health, mind, body, and soul,
Invest in yourself, always aim to grow,
Read, learn, and be curious, my dear son,
For knowledge opens doors, and life has begun.
Cherish your relationships, family, and friends,
Create lasting bonds that will never bend,
Love deeply, and cherish those around you,
For it's the love that makes life feel new.
And in the moments of doubt and sorrow,
Remember that tomorrow brings a new tomorrow,
So hold your head up high with pride,
And let every challenge be your guide.
Life may not always be fair,
But know that I'll always be there,
To offer you my love, my strength, and my care,

For you're both my sons and my heart will forever bear
In fruit from being involved in your youth

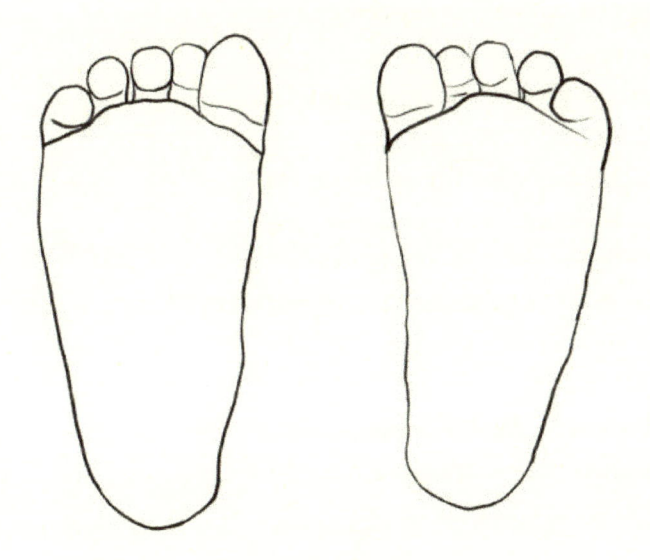

IF WE HAVE A DAUGHTER SOMEDAY.
Dear Daughter, as you journey through life,
I offer you words of wisdom to guide,
Some pearls of advice to help you thrive,
And live a life of joy, love, and pride.
Set your sights high, and dream big dreams,
Strive for excellence, wherever it may lead,
And when the road ahead is rough and steep,
Remember that your strength will be your keep.
Never lose sight of who you are,
Let your heart shine bright like a star,
Be true to yourself, and follow your heart,
For that's where your deepest passions start.
Don't be afraid to take chances, my dear,
Embrace every experience, rise above your fear,
Take risks and explore, push past your comfort zone,
For that's where the greatest learning is grown.
Love yourself, my dear, just as you are,
With all your flaws, your quirks, your scars,
You're beautiful inside and out, my dear,
And to me, you'll always be lovable and near.
Respect others and value their worth,
Walk in compassion, kindness, and mirth,
Be a source of joy, be a light of hope,
And with every smile, you'll touch lives and cope.
Build lasting relationships, dear daughter of mine,
With friends, family, and a love divine,
Cherish the moments, hold them close and true,
And let the bonds of love carry you through,
Dear daughter, it's your life, your journey to take,
But always know, my love will never forsake,
You're a treasure to me, my greatest delight,

And in my heart, you'll always shine bright.

LESSONS FROM CHRONIC PAIN.
You don't need to be anywhere specific to be successful, never sell out
You only need to keep moving past doubt
Life may revolve around money but it's meanings are rooted deeper than digits
Don't age to become resentful or bitter
When the experiences you've had?
No one else may have and the lessons from that can be even sweeter
Respect everyone you encounter because each person can be a father, mother, sister or brother
The tales they have from what they've overcome is where your wisdom has begun
We're all children yet the experience is what graduates us to elders
Be proud of yourself no matter how this life turns out

## WE'VE COME FAR.

I've written out this heart when cold showed me it was heart less
I was left out long enough to become guilty enough of showing my heart less
Yes I've been mean, I've screamed and have threatened
I'm no monster but it's what you can turn to when pain keeps you in its vice grip longer
It makes the light in your life so much dimmer
But now it's time to retire and learn how to rest
Even when the pressures of life doesn't ease
Don't ever feel like you're being squeezed too hard
Lets all look back and acknowledge we've come from far

NEW FAMILY.
Family, the bond that ties us all,
A love that stands through rise and fall,
Through thick and thin, they have our back,
Their love unwavering, never slack.
They pick us up when we are down,
And stand with us through every frown,
Supporting us through every strife,
And holding us through every life.
Their love, a shield that keeps us strong,
A source of joy, a lifelong song,
Their presence a calming balm,
Weathering every emotional storm.
Family, the anchor of our being,
A love that's true, forever freeing,
They are the ones we hold so dear,
And their love, we'll forever revere.

PERSEVEERANCE.
In this life, I've tried my best,
Striving hard to blaze a path,
Through good times, and through the rest,
Fought through pain, and feel God's wrath.
The road has been rough, sometimes steep,
But always, I've tried to climb,
Through pain and hurt, I refused to weep,
For my family, I gave my prime.
I've worked hard, day and night,
To put food on the table each day,
To provide for my kids, keep them tight,
And hold my wife, come what may.
The journey has been long and tough,
And often, I felt like giving in,
But I persevered, like the warrior rough,
Fought battles out of loss, and always win.
My love for my family, wells my soul,
Gives me the strength to carry on,
And when I think I've lost my goal,
Their love reignites my dawn.
Through all the storms, and all the strife,
I kept pushing, holding firm to my vows,
For my family, I'd gladly give my life,
They are the light that leads me now.
Dear God, I thank you for this chance,
To love my family, to show them care,
To provide for them, in every circumstance,
And be the rock, on which they can bear.
So as I look back on my life,
I see trials, battles, and scars,
But in my heart, there's no strife,

For I have won, through God's stars.
The essence of love, it fills the air

LOVE IN THE AIR.
A fragrance sweet, beyond compare
It whispers in the trees at night
And dances in the morning light
It's in the laughter of a child
And in the tears of a heart gone wild
It binds us together, one and all
And catches us if ever we fall
It's a warm embrace on a cold day
A gentle touch to chase the pain away
It's the light in the darkest hour
And the hope when there seems no power
It's the bond that brings us hand in hand
A strength that only love can command
It's the grace that lifts us up above
The very essence of true love
For where love is, there is no fear
No doubt, no hurt, nowhere near
Just a feeling pure and bright
That fills our hearts with joyous light
So let us cherish this gift, so rare
And spread its essence everywhere
For in the end, when all is done
Love is all that we will have won

FOREVER AND ALWAYS.
My dear sweet wife, my heart's delight
You are my sun, my shining light
Your beauty radiates from inside
Filling my heart with love and pride
Your eyes, they sparkle like the stars
Your smile, it melts away my scars
You are the reason for my life

My love for you, it knows no strife
Your touch, it gives me wings to fly
Your embrace, it makes me want to try
To be a better man each day
To cherish you in every way
You are the treasure of my heart
With you by my side, I'll never be apart
I love you more than words can say
My dear sweet wife, forever and always

## GRANDPARENTHOOD.

Oh, the joy that fills my heart
When I think of a brand new start
A little one to love and hold
A grandchild whose story will unfold
The thought of seeing my child as a parent
Fills me with delight and excitement
To watch them grow and learn to care
For a precious life so innocent and rare
I hope to teach and guide them well
To share the stories that I have to tell
And together we'll create new memories
To cherish forever, to the highest degrees
So I wait with patience and with hope
For that special moment that will elope
And bring me the gift of grandparenthood
A blessing that truly feels so good.

LEGACY.

Death is one of the most complex, mysterious, and spiritually rich phenomena that humans encounter in their lives. From the spiritual standpoint, death is viewed not as an end, but as a transition from one state of being to another.

Mystics and spiritual leaders from different traditions speak of death as a passage that leads to a new reality, a new dimension of consciousness, where the soul resides and experiences the afterlife. Death is seen as an initiation, a journey into the unknown, where the soul is purified, and the spirit is elevated.

In many traditions, death is viewed as an opportunity for transformation and spiritual evolution. As the physical body dies, the soul is liberated from the physical constraints and limitations. It is believed that the soul continues to exist in the afterlife in a form that is more refined and pure, and that it retains all of the memories, experiences, and emotions that it accumulated during its physical existence.

From a spiritual standpoint, death is not an end, but a new beginning, a new phase of existence that leads to greater awareness, enlightenment, and unity with the divine. It is believed that through the process of death and the afterlife, the soul is able to achieve a level of spiritual growth and understanding that is not attainable in the physical world.

Death is viewed as an essential aspect of the natural cycle of life, a part of the order of the universe. It is believed that the soul chooses the time, place, and circumstances of its physical death based on its level of consciousness and the lessons that it needs to learn in order to evolve. The soul understands that death is merely a transition and embraces it as a necessary part of the journey.

In conclusion, from a spiritual standpoint, death is not a tragedy, but an essential aspect of the natural cycle of life. It is a journey that leads to new states of being and greater awareness. It is an opportunity for transformation, evolution, and spiritual growth. As we embrace death,

we can learn to appreciate life more fully, and we can gain a deeper understanding of the spiritual nature of our existence.
We wont live forever but we can show unending love together
And this is truly how life goes on forever.

VOW.
I may not be the greatest husband,
But I want to be the one you adore.
I try my best to make you happy,
But sometimes I fall short, I know.
I may forget your favorite flowers,
Or the way you like your coffee just so,
But I promise you, my love,
My heart is in the right place, you know.
I may not always listen as I should,
Or show you the attention you deserve,
But I vow to be a better man,
And make your happiness my top concern.
I'll cook you dinner with love,
And give you massages after a long day,
I'll be the shoulder to cry on,
And the voice that guides you on your way.
I may not be perfect, my love,
But I will always strive to be,
For you are my heart and soul,
And I want to be the best husband for thee.

Milton Keynes UK
Ingram Content Group UK Ltd.
UKHW031213111124
451035UK00007B/736